Celebrate
the Spirit

THE OLYMPIC GAMES

Celebrate the Spirit

the Spirit

THE OLYMPIC GAMES

CLEVE DHEENSAW & **DEANNA BINDER**

ORCA BOOK PUBLISHERS

1996

To Jeanette King, Peter Spear and the leaders of the Calgary Olympic Winter Games Organizing Committee who believed that the Olympic spirit could and should inspire young people. They have made this Olympic odyssey possible. And to my husband, Alf, and our son, Stephen, who believed in me. With thanks.

D.B.

For my little Olympians, Brittany and Casey.

C.D.

Canadian Cataloguing in Publication Data

Dheensaw, Cleve, 1956–
Celebrate the spirit

Includes index.
ISBN 1-55143-066-3

1. Olympics—History. I. Binder, Deanna. II. Title.
GV721.5.D53 1996   796.48   C95-911174-3

Design by Arifin Graham, Alaris Design
Publication assistance provided by The Canada Council
Photography credits: All-Sport, Sporting Spotlights,
    Deanna Binder Collection, Canadian Sport Images
Printed and bound in Hong Kong

Orca Book Publishers
PO Box 5626, Station B
Victoria, BC   V8R 6S4
Canada

Orca Book Publishers
PO Box 468
Custer, WA   98240-0468
USA

10 9 8 7 6 5 4 3 2 1

Front cover photos: *Top:* Linford Christie of Britain wins 100 m at the Barcelona Olympics. *Bottom (from left):* Gary Honey of Australia leaps to long jump silver at '84 L.A. Olympics; Canadian Olympic rowing hero Silken Laumann *(courtesy Canadian Sport Images, Ted Grant)*; Charles Barkley and David Robinson of the U.S. Dream Team at Barcelona '92.
Back cover photos: *(from left):* Kathy Read swims at the '92 Barcelona Olympics *(courtesy Canadian Sport Images, Ted Grant)*; Sebastian Coe wins the 1500 m at the '94 L.A. Olympics; the Josephson twins win silver in sychronized swimming duets in Barcelona *(courtesy Canadian Sport Images, Ted Grant)*; Skier Kate Pace shows her form at the '94 Lillehammer Games *(courtesy Canadian Sport Images, Claus Anderson)*.

Table of Contents

Celebrate the Spirit: The Olympic Games

One hundred years ago in 1896, 311 athletes from thirteen countries travelled to Athens, Greece for the first Olympic Games of the modern era. From those humble beginnings, the Olympic Games have grown into a celebration of sport unequalled anywhere.

Every four years the Games bring together the best athletes in the world for the world's greatest sporting event. In 1996 in Atlanta, there will be over 10,000 athletes from 190 countries participating in the Games. And perhaps hundreds of millions of people will watch them on television.

The Olympic spirit — the spirit of friendly but fierce competition — ignites the hopes and dreams of people on every continent. It creates a world-wide Olympic family whose members come together in peace, to compete and to share their friendship and their way of life.

That competitive spirit echoes the spirit of the citizens of the city-states of ancient Greece who also sent their best athletes to compete in the original Games in ancient Olympia.

That Competitive Spirit!

Charlotte Cooper won a gold medal in a tennis event for women in 1900. She became the first female Olympic gold medalist.

NOW

Jason rolled over again. He just couldn't sleep. Tomorrow was his big race. He'd run with his parents in every 10 km run in town. He'd run around the block twelve times every day. He'd run around the school grounds ten times every noon hour for months. He thought he was the best runner in town. But he didn't know for sure. There was a new guy down the street. Maybe he was better. Maybe he didn't feel as jittery. Maybe he, too, expected to win.

The prize for winning the local cross-country race was tickets to the national championship football game. And Jason was a football fan. He'd never be able to afford those tickets himself. He just had to win!

Spiridon Louis won the first marathon race in the first of the modern Oympic Games in Athens in 1896.

The modern Olympic Games are celebrating a birthday. They are 100 years old.

Sebastion Coe of Britain wins the men's 1500 m at the 1984 Los Angeles Olympics.

Athletes in the
ancient Olympic
Games won a crown
of olive leaves.

THEN

On another continent in another time, another Jason rolled over again. He was sleeping in a tent on the plain of ancient Olympia, waiting for the sun to rise on his big race. His father, who was a former Olympic champion, was still sound asleep beside him. "I'll never be as good as he is," worried Jason.

Father and son had come hundreds of miles by boat and on foot to compete in the Olympic Games. Jason had trained for months under close supervision. Only the very best were allowed to compete in front of the thousands of spectators who always showed up for the Games. He had even had to be in Olympia a whole month early to train under official Olympic trainers.

He knew he was one of the best of the racers in the boys' event. But was he good enough to win?

"Watch Mito of Sparta," his father said as they lined up to enter the stadium. "Let him take the early lead. He burns himself out early. Stay on his heels and come up from behind for the finish. You can beat him then."

Jason wasn't so sure, but he was going to give it everything he had. He was on his own in his first Olympic competition.

View of the sacred grove at Olympia, Greece. The flame is first lit here before each Olympic Games and then transported thousands of miles to the host city.

Where the Olympic Spirit Began: Ancient Olympia

NOW

If Jason were to visit Olympia today, he'd find a small town whose main street is lined with jewelry and souvenir shops. He'd walk around a large field nearby, strewn with old stones, and half-standing marble columns. He'd still be able to have a race with a friend up and down the old track, but the grassy slopes on either side would be empty. The only sounds he'd hear would be the click of the cameras of other tourists and the gentle sighing of a, thank goodness, cool wind in the grasses near the river bank. In Greece, summers can be raging hot.

Jason might then look up to the tree-covered hill of Kronus, which rises right beside the ruins. Maybe someone would tell him that from the top the athletes of the ancient Games honored the sun god, Apollo, who drove his flaming chariot over the distant mountains. That hill is a tough climb early in the morning.

If Jason was lucky, someone would describe the buildings that stood where he now could see only the outlines of a wall or a platform. Someone else might even have a picture of what it probably looked like in the days when that other Jason won his Olympic wreath of olive leaves, and became a hero in his city.

The site of the ancient Olympic Games lay buried under 4.5 m of silt for 1,300 years.

Athletes in the ancient Games had to train in Olympia under supervision for four weeks before the competitions.

THEN

On this day in the sacred sanctuary of ancient Olympia, everyone waits for sunrise. Already there is a bustle of activity on the roads leading to the stadium. Spectators want a good viewing site on the stadium's grassy slopes. Salesmen and entertainers of every type want to make sure they have a good location to display their wares or talents. They all crowd into the confusion of temples, training facilities, hotels, official buildings and statues that crowd the site. Jason and his father join them.

The big temple looms over everything. Olympia is a religious site — has been for a thousand years. Many goddesses and gods have had a special home in Olympia. The original temple was built in honor of Hera, the mother goddess. Right now, however, it is Zeus who is all powerful. The five days of the Olympic Games are held in his honor. His temple, with its hundreds of marble pillars, is the biggest building around.

As they walk past the temple to the stadium, Jason reflects on the religious ceremonies he has already experienced. He can't help thinking that the priests were awfully long-winded. He really just wanted to get on with his training, but the religious ceremonies are an important activity for athletes as well as spectators. If he was going to do his best, he figured he'd better be on the good side of the god.

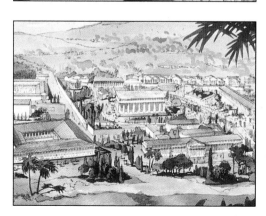

The glories of ancient Greece, the birthplace of the Olympics.

The ancient Olympics were held every four years.

The ancient Games went on for 1,000 years.

Ancient Olympic Trivia: You Asked

Where is Olympia?

In Greece, near the west coast of the big peninsula.

When were the earliest recorded Olympic Games?

In 776 B.C. (That's 2,770 years ago!)

How many people could watch?

40,000 (But only men; women were not allowed to watch or compete. They had their own Games at another time.)

What did they win?

A crown of olive leaves.

   Are you kidding? No…the crown of leaves was considered a gift of the god. Remember, the Games were a religious activity. But any Olympic Games winner became a hero in his city and lived pretty well for the rest of his life.

What did they wear?

Nothing.

   Are you kidding? No…spectators as well as athletes participated with no clothes on. Nobody is quite sure why, but the rumor is that a woman sneaked in once, and after that, anybody entering the stadium had to leave their clothes in their tents.

What sports did they have?

Turn the page…

What happened to the Games during wars?

Nothing. They carried on. A special truce was declared before and after each Games, and people attending were usually granted safe passage through other city-states.

When did they end?

In 393 A.D. — which is about 1,600 years ago. Can you believe it? The ancient Olympic Games took place every four years in the same place for over one thousand years.

Why did the Olympic Games end?

The great Greek city-states like Athens and Sparta started to fight among themselves. They thus became sitting ducks for a conquest by a military genius from a city in northern Greece. His name was Alexander the Great. Then the Romans from the peninsula now called Italy conquered them. Neither Alexander nor the Romans understood the traditional values of the Games, although they were enthusiastic competitors.

Soon the Games didn't resemble the old Games at all. Cheating occurred more often; athletes started to compete for bigger and bigger amounts of money (sound familiar?). The Games lost their religious significance and their important values. The new Christian emperors did not support an athletic event dedicated to a former Greek god. One of them sent his soldiers to wreck the site. Earthquakes and floods finished the job. The ancient buildings lay buried for hundreds of years.

Sports of the Ancient Games

FOOT RACES

Athletes didn't run around a track. They ran straight from the starting line to a post about 200 m down the track. They then did a quick turnaround and ran back. The 200 m distance was called a "stade." Guess where our word "stadium" comes from?

HORSE RACES

Nero, a kooky emperor of Rome, once declared himself a winner in the famous Olympic chariot race by ordering all other competitors to be disqualified. Nice guy? No wonder the Games were cancelled soon after.

PENTATHLON (long jump, javelin, discus, a foot race and wrestling)

Long jumpers jumped from a standing start and used weights to help them increase their distance. The weights were dropped as they came down for the landing. Javelin throwers used a thong attached to the spear and hooked through a finger to increase the distance of their throw.

BOXING

Boxers wore thongs wrapped around their hands and wrists. In Roman times the thongs were reinforced with iron or lead grommets, making them deadly weapons. Boxers fought until one of them signalled defeat by raising one or two fingers or fell to the ground unconscious.

WRESTLING

Upright wrestlers had to throw their opponent three times from a standing position. Ground wrestlers competed in a muddy pit, making the holds difficult.

PANKRATION

Pankration was a combination of boxing and wrestling with anything allowed except the use of nails and teeth. It was always dangerous. One athlete, while being strangled, managed to crush and dislocate the ankle of his opponent. Although he died, he won the victory, because his opponent, unable to stand the pain, had signalled defeat.

What the ancient Greek Olympics might have looked like to Jason.

The Modern Olympic Games: Birth of a Family

Baron Pierre de Coubertin.

One hundred years ago, people in Europe were finding out about the ruins of ancient Olympia, and about the values and sports of those athletic events of long ago. A few of them got together to form a committee to organize a sporting event for young men from different countries. They called their event the Olympic Games. The first Games were held in 1896, in Athens, the capitol city of Greece.

The man who became the leader of the new Olympic Games organization was Pierre de Coubertin from France. He called his committee the International Olympic Committee. The IOC is still in charge today.

Baron Pierre de Coubertin believed that young people could build their characters, minds and bodies through sport. This was quite a new idea back in the late 1800s.

De Coubertin thought sport could also help foster world peace. If nations were too busy competing in sports, they wouldn't have time for war. He was wrong, of course. But that was his dream.

When de Coubertin was just a teenager, German archaeologists had dug up the ancient city of Olympia, Greece, and many artifacts from the ancient Olympic Games were found. De Coubertin was greatly inspired by this. Why not a modern Olympics? he thought.

He was so enthusiastic about this idea that he convinced a group of sports people from thirteen nations meeting in 1894 at Paris that a modern Olympics would be a good thing. And what better place than Greece to hold the first modern Games? De Coubertin wanted the first Games to go to Olympia itself, site of the ancient Greek Games. The stadium at Olympia was found but was far too old. So Athens was chosen.

The 2,000-year-old ruins of the ancient stadium in Athens were rebuilt in marble. The first Games of the modern era were held in 1896 at Athens.

As for de Coubertin, he loved the Olympic Games so much that when he died in 1937, his heart was taken out of his body and put into a marble column in front of the eternal Olympic flame in Olympia. You can go and visit it when you are in Greece. You could say that de Coubertin put his whole heart into the Olympics.

The Olympic Family Grows:
Cities That Have Hosted an Olympic Games

THE GAMES OF THE OLYMPIAD

#	Date	City	Countries	Competitors
1	1896	Athens	13	311
2	1900	Paris	22	1,330
3	1904	St. Louis	13	625
4	1908	London	22	2,056
5	1912	Stockholm	28	2,546
6	1916	Not celebrated		
7	1920	Antwerp	29	2,692
8	1924	Paris	44	3,092
9	1928	Amsterdam	46	3,014
10	1932	Los Angeles	37	1,408
11	1936	Berlin	49	4,066
12	1940	Not celebrated		
13	1944	Not celebrated		
14	1948	London	59	4,099
15	1952	Helsinki	69	4,925
16	1956	Melbourne	67	3,342
17	1960	Rome	83	5,348
18	1964	Tokyo	93	5,140
19	1968	Mexico City	112	5,530
20	1972	Munich	122	7,156
21	1976	Montreal	92	6,085
22	1980	Moscow	81	5,326
23	1984	Los Angeles	140	7,078
24	1988	Seoul	159	8,465
25	1992	Barcelona	171	10,632
26	1996	Atlanta		
27	2000	Sydney		

THE OLYMPIC WINTER GAMES

#	Date	City	Countries	Competitors
1	1924	Chamonix	16	258
2	1928	St. Moritz	25	464
3	1932	Lake Placid	17	252
4	1936	Garmisch-Partenkirchen	28	668
5	1948	St. Moritz	28	669
6	1952	Oslo	30	694
7	1956	Cortina d'Ampezzo	32	820
8	1960	Squaw Valley	30	665
9	1964	Innsbruck	36	1,091
10	1968	Grenoble	37	1,158
11	1972	Sapporo	35	1,006
12	1976	Innsbruck	37	1,123
13	1980	Lake Placid	37	1,072
14	1984	Sarajevo	49	1,274
15	1988	Calgary	57	1,425
16	1992	Albertville	64	1,801
17	1994	Lillehammer	67	1,738
18	1998	Nagano		
19	2002	Salt Lake City		

Posters from (top left and clockwise) the 1920 Antwerp, 1928 Amsterdam and 1936 Berlin summer olympics and the 1956 Cortina d'Ampezzo Winter Olympics.

Olympic Family Traditions

There are five Olympic rings, representing the five continents. The rings are colored (from left) blue, yellow, black, green and red. The colors are symbolic in that at least one of those colors appears in the flag of every nation in the world.

OLYMPIC RINGS

Everyone recognizes the five Olympic rings. They symbolize the highest level of excellence in sport throughout the world. They also represent the ideals and goals of the Olympic movement, which have inspired people for more than a hundred years. The colors of the top three rings are blue, black and red (right to left). The bottom rings are yellow and green.

THE OLYMPIC FLAG

The five colored rings, blue, black, red, yellow and green, on a pure white background make up the Olympic flag. In an Olympic city, the Olympic flag must be flown where other flags are flown, and displayed prominently on a pole in the middle of the stadium.

THE OLYMPIC MOTTO

Citius, Altius, Fortius which means Swifter, Higher, Stronger.

THE OLYMPIC FLAME

The Olympic flame begins its journey to an Olympic Games in ancient Olympia, Greece, near the spot where competitors lined up to enter the ancient stadium. There the light of the sun reflecting off a mirror lights oil in a sacred cauldron, and from this fire, the first torch is lit. The torch makes its way to the Olympic Games in a torch relay organized by the city hosting the Games. During the opening ceremonies of the Games, the last runner lights a huge cauldron in the Olympic stadium.

THE CEREMONIES OF THE GAMES

It is an Olympic family tradition that every opening ceremony include a parade of athletes from each participating country, the raising of the Olympic flag, the lighting of the Olympic flame, and the reciting of the Olympic oath by an athlete and a judge. In the parade of athletes, Greece always enters first in honor of its heritage as the home of the ancient Olympic Games and the first host of an Olympic Games (1896) in the modern era. The host country enters last.

Medals are presented to first, second and third place winners during a ceremony which includes the playing of the national anthem of the winning country and the raising of the flags of the first, second and third place winners.

Closing ceremonies include the lowering of the Olympic flag, the extinguishing of the flame and a march from the arena by the athletes as a whole group and not by nation. This symbolizes a world-wide camaraderie of athletes.

The official Olympic flag, here being carried in during the opening ceremonies of the 1976 Montreal Summer Olympics, flies in the main stadium for the duration of each Olympics. It is lowered during the closing ceremonies and passed on to the mayor of the next host city.

The flame burns during the opening ceremonies in the 1988 Seoul Summer Olympics.

Decorating for an Olympic Games: *Mascots, Logos and Posters*

London took on the task of restarting the Olympics after the horror of World War II. Here is a poster from those 1948 Summer Games.

A poster for the 1992 Albertville Winter Olympics drawn by a French child.

Poster from the 1928 Winter Olympics in St. Moritz, Switzerland.

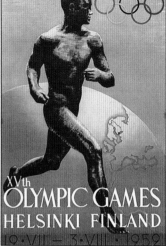

The official logo of the 1988 Seoul Summer Olympics.

The plucky Finns, with only a small country, a few resources and little money, successfully hosted the 1952 Summer Olympics in Helsinki.

The official mascot of the 1980 Moscow Games was a bear named Misha.

Athletics

Primitive people learned very early to run fast, jump high and throw far. Their survival depended upon it. Today's athletic (track and field) events are based on these ancient skills. Throughout most of the world, these events are called athletics. In North America they are called track and field. Most Olympic races take place on a 400 m oval track. The throwing and jumping competitions take place on the infield. This allows spectators to watch a number of track and field competitions taking place at the same time.

Running events include:
- *sprints:* where a runner explodes from the start and maintains top speed for 100 m, 200 m and 400 m races. Sprints are run in lanes.
- *middle distance races:* which include 800 m, 1500 m, 3000 m and 5000 m races. Middle distance runners need to have the strength of the sprinter and the physical conditioning of the long-distance runner. Middle distance events take place around the 400 m track. Runners maneuver for position, and tactics are important.
- *long-distance races:* The 10,000 m race takes place on the track. The marathon is a 42.195 km race that starts and finishes on the track, but winds through the roads near the stadium.
- *relays:* which include 4 X 100 m and 4 X 400 m races. Good relay racing involves a fast team and accurate baton passing.

Superstar Carl Lewis of the U.S. in the long jump at the Barcelona Olympics.

A shot is not thrown; it is pushed off the shoulder.

In pole vault today's poles are custom-made according to the vaulter's weight. They act a little bit like catapults.

- *hurdles:* Hurdlers sprint, then jump over small gates. They try to keep their rhythm as smooth as possible.
- *steeplechase:* which is a 3000 m race through an obstacle course. In each lap around the track the runner jumps four hurdles and a water jump.
- *walks:* where competitors must maintain unbroken contact with the ground.

Maybe they were inspired by the high speed that kangaroos can reach. The Australian women were the fastest in the world at the 1952 Helsinki and 1956 Melbourne Olympics. They won all six gold medals during those two Games in the women's 100 m and 200 m sprints and 80 m hurdles. Marjorie Jackson won 100 m and 200 m gold in 1952 and Betty Cuthbert did the same in 1956. Shirley Strickland took bronze in the 100 m in 1952 and Marlene Mathews won bronze in both the 100 m and 200 m in 1956. Strickland, a college lecturer, won gold in the explosive and fast 80 m hurdles in both the 1952 and 1956 Games and finished her career with a total of seven Olympic medals.

Australia's speed in women's track continued in the 1960s when Raelene Boyle won three silver medals in the 100 m and 200 m at the 1968 Mexico City and 1972 Munich Olympics. She was unlucky not to win another three Olympic medals when she finished fourth in the 100 m at Mexico City in 1968 and Montreal in 1976 and was disqualified in the 200 m at Montreal for two false starts.

Everybody laughed at Dick Fosbury's high jumping style. The American ran to the bar and then turned his back to it as he leaped over. The year was 1968 and people considered Fosbury's methods very strange. Everybody else at the time jumped over the bar frontwards. People laughed at Fosbury and said he would not go far with his bizarre style. Who had ever heard of such a thing? People joked about him and called his jumping style the Fosbury Flop. But he was no flop. He won the gold medal at the Mexico City Olympics. Now, almost all the high jumpers in the world use the Fosbury Flop. So Dick was hardly a flop.

A man's discus weights 2 kg; a woman's weighs 1 kg.

Jumping events include:

- *long jump:* which involves a running take-off from a board and a leap into a sand-filled landing area.
- *triple jump:* which is sometimes known as the hop, step and jump.
- *high jump:* over a crossbar suspended between two rigid uprights.
- *pole vault:* where competitors use a flexible pole to help them vault over a crossbar supported on two uprights.

If you win a gold medal for a small country, expect to be treated like a conquering hero and have lots of things named after you. Hasely Crawford of Trinidad and Tobago was the unexpected winner of the men's 100 m gold medal in track and field at the 1976 Montreal Summer Olympics. The people in Trinidad and Tobago were so thrilled and excited by that feat they treated Crawford like a king when he returned home. He had a stamp minted in his honor and a British West Indies Airlines jet named after him. Maybe someday if you fly on BWI airlines, you'll be on the plane named *Hasely Crawford*. There were also many calypso songs written about Crawford in Trinidad and Tobago. If you ever go there, you'll probably hear them being sung.

The old Iron Curtain was lifted by the power of love at the 1956 Melbourne Olympics. The gold medalist hammer thrower, big Hal Connolly of the U.S., fell in love watching women's discus gold medalist Olga Fikotova of Czechoslovakia during her practice throws. He asked her out and they went on a date in the Athletes Village. They decided to get married. But not everybody liked that idea — especially the Communists who ran Fikotova's country back then. But the two lovebirds appealed directly to the president of Czechoslovakia. He said okay. The two were married in Prague the following year and moved to California. They competed together in three more Olympics. They had four children. And they always remembered their first date in Melbourne.

Throwing events include:

- *discus*
- *javelin*
- *shot put*
- *hammer throw*

Stella Walsh was an American resident who ran for Poland, using the name Stanislawa Walasiewicz. She won the Olympic gold medal in the women's 100 m at Los Angeles in 1932 and the silver medal in that event at Berlin in 1936. But it was revealed in 1980 that Walsh was actually a man! He had fooled everybody in the Olympics and won two medals in a women's event.

Decathlon and Heptathlon:

Men compete in the decathlon, ten events over two days. The decathalon events are the 100 m, 400 m and 1500 m runs, as well as 100 m hurdles, high jump, long jump, pole vault, discus, javelin and shot put.

Women compete in heptathlon, seven events, also over two days. The events of heptathlon are 200 m and 800 m runs, 100 m hurdles, high jump, long jump, shot put and javelin throw.

Murray Halberg of New Zealand overcame great odds and is an excellent example of why you should never give up. When he was seventeen years old, his shoulder and arm were severely damaged in a rugby game. Halberg had to learn how to dress, write and feed himself all over again as if he were a baby. But he never gave up. His useless arm would just flap by his side, so he could no longer play rugby. But he turned to running. Exactly ten years after he lost the use of his arm, Halberg won the gold medal in the 5000 m at the 1960 Rome Olympics.

Great timing is needed in the relay races. Here Carl Lewis of the U.S. receives the baton in the men's 4 X 100 m relay at the 1992 Barcelona Summer Olympics. The U.S. team won the gold medal in a world record 37.40 seconds. That's fast!

The great Kip Keino of Kenya led at this point in the men's 1500 m final of the 1972 Munich Olympics, but Pekka Vasala of Finland (in blue) would overtake him for the gold medal. Nevertheless Kip still won two golds and two silvers in his Olympic career and three golds and a bronze in the Commonwealth Games.

Little Hezekiah Kipchoge Keino was only ten years old when he was walking down a road in Kenya. All of a sudden he turned a corner and there was a leopard. The leopard was eating a goat.

The big black leopard got up on its legs and looked at little Kip Keino. Little Kip backed away from the leopard and turned and ran.

He never looked back. He just kept running until he got home.

About a year later, little Kip was again walking along the same road when he was grabbed by highway robbers who tried to steal his pennies. But Kip managed to wriggle loose and he ran away so fast that the robbers couldn't catch him. The robbers were no match for his speed. Nor were many of Kip's opponents on the track. The little boy who ran away from leopards and robbers on that dusty road in Kenya kept running. He ran so long and so hard that he won the gold medal in the 1500 m and silver in the 5000 m at the 1968 Mexico City Olympics and the gold in the steeplechase and silver in the 1500 m at the 1972 Munich Olympics.

Women first competed in an Olympic marathon in 1984.

Fred Lorz of New York looked to be the winner of the marathon at the 1904 St. Louis Olympics. Officials were about to give him his gold medal when they found out that Lorz had actually ridden in a car for about twelve miles of the race. That's called the lazy way to win an Olympic gold. Lorz was disqualified and the gold medal went to Thomas Hicks, who had lost ten pounds while running the marathon without hitching a ride.

Aquatics: *swimming, diving, synchronized swimming*

Aqua means water. Athletes in aquatic sports race or perform in or over the water. Swimmers race through the water using different body strokes. Divers do twists and somersaults over the water from diving boards of different heights. Synchronized swimmers do acrobatic patterns in the water in time to music.

Olympic swimmers compete in freestyle, breaststroke, backstroke, butterfly and relay races. There is also a race with laps using each of the different strokes called the individual medley. Great swimmers perfect their starts off the blocks and their turns at the end of a lap.

Cave drawings 11,000 years old show swimmers in Libya, Africa.

Swimming lessons were offered in Egypt as early as 2200 B.C.

Women first competed in Olympic swimming events in 1912.

Women swimmers at the 1912 Stokholm Olympics, the first year women's aquatics events were held in the Games

The city of Barcelona provided a magnificent backdrop for Olympic diving in 1992.

High over the pool an Olympic diver breathes deeply and begins her run-up. Lifting off the 10 m board she completes two somersaults and a half-twist before aiming straight as an arrow for the water. In the next couple of days she will also compete from a 3 m springboard. She couldn't count the number of times she has landed badly in the water while practising a new move. Her courage and her determination to "nail a dive" will eventually make her an Olympic champion.

Different dives are created by combining the six different groups of dives with different body positions. The groups are: forward, backward, reverse, inward, twist and armstand. The body positions are: straight, pike, tuck and free. Each dive is assigned a degree of difficulty, which is taken into consideration in the final score for a dive.

Diving was first held in the Olympic Games of 1904.

When Anthony Nesty won the gold medal in the men's 100 m butterfly at the 1988 Seoul Summer Olympics, he became the first black person ever to win an Olympic swimming medal and the first person ever from the nation of Suriname, a former Dutch colony on the northern coast of South America, to win an Olympic medal in any sport. He was treated like a king when he returned to his homeland as thousands of people lined the streets for a special parade to greet their nation's first Olympic medalist. Nesty got a stamp printed in his honor and gold coins were minted with his face on them. The largest stadium in the country was renamed the Anthony Nesty Stadium.

The young women in the pool in their red sequined hats and suits smile at the crowd as they conclude their routine. They know they performed in perfect unison this time, and they expect good marks from the judges. As synchronized swimmers, they receive marks for how they perform a set of compulsory figures in the water, and then for a swimming routine performed to music. They have to hold their breath for up to sixty seconds in some of their more difficult underwater moves. As much as half of their current routine is performed upside down in the pool. They are on their way to becoming Olympic champions.

Fast Olympic 50 m pools have deep gutters on the sides and ropes between the lanes to reduce waves. Early Olympic swimmers were not so lucky. The swimmers in the three events in Athens in 1896 competed in the sea and battled cold water and choppy waves. In France in 1900 they swam with the current in the Seine River. Their records were not counted because they had an advantage.

The breaststroke was used for the endurance races that were popular in Europe in the 1800s.

Synchronized swimming has moves called swordfish, porpoise, heron and albatross.

The butterfly is the most exhausting stroke in the Olympics.

Backstroke was added to the Olympic Games in 1912 at the Stockholm Olympic Games.

The crawl (or freestyle) stroke was an invention of native American Indians who thrashed the water with their arms, like sails of a windmill. They looked like they were "crawling" over the water said one journalist. Since it was the fastest stroke, Olympic competitors usually chose it for the freestyle events, and it was renamed freestyle.

Winner Alex Baumann of Canada (left), silver medalist Pablo Morales of the U.S. (center) and bronze medalist Neil Cochran of Britain wave to the crowd after the men's 200 m individual medley swim final at the 1984 Los Angeles Olympics.

"Me Tarzan. You Jane."

From Olympic swimming hero to Tarzan, the Ape Man. That was Johnny Weissmuller. He won three individual gold medals in swimming at the 1924 Paris Olympics and two more at the Amsterdam Games in 1928. His big body was noticed by Hollywood producers when they saw him modeling swimsuits in a magazine ad. They said: "Hey, this Olympic champion should be in the movies. He is so big and handsome. People will pay money to see him on the big screen."

And they did. Weissmuller made twelve Tarzan movies and was like Indiana Jones when your grandparents were growing up. Weissmuller was once playing golf in Cuba in 1959 when Fidel Castro's rebels came on the course and arrested him with guns. Weissmuller let out the Tarzan yell and beat his chest with his hands. The surprised rebels said "It's Tarzan, it's Tarzan" and put down their guns and let Weissmuller continue with his golf game.

Hollywood producers loved big Olympic athletes for their Tarzan movies. Three other Olympic medalists — Buster Crabbe, Glenn Morris and Herman Brix — also went on to play Tarzan in the movies.

From the open water of the Bay of Zea near the Greek port of Piraeus in 1896 to the state-of-the-art 1996 Olympic Pool at Georgia Tech University in Atlanta, swimming has been a part of every Summer Olympics of the modern era.

Dawn Fraser of Australia was one of the greatest swimmers the world has ever seen. She won a total of five gold medals and three silvers at the Olympics. She fought her way to the 1964 Tokyo Olympics after she was involved in a horrible car accident in which her mother was killed. Dawn overcame her grief and her own injuries to win a gold and silver at Tokyo.

Fraser was a high-spirited girl who liked to play pranks. One night, as a joke, she swam across the moat of the Imperial Palace and stole the Japanese Emperor's flag. Fortunately the Emperor got the joke and let Dawn keep the flag. Unfortuantely Australian swimming officials were not so happy and banned Dawn for ten years. That ban was later reduced to four years.

Gymnastics

Gymnasts do somersaults, twists, turns, leaps and acrobatics on all different kinds of apparatus, demonstrating their incredible strength, balance and control. The men perform on parallel bars, horizontal bars, pommel horse and rings and do vaults over a box horse. Women perform on the uneven bars and balance beam and do vaults over a box horse. Both men and women compete on a mat in floor exercises. The men's floor exercises must include a variety of tumbling skills with turns, leaps, balances and momentary poses. The women's exercises are accompanied by music and combine dance, tumbling and acrobatic movements.

Rhythmic gymnasts strive to balance natural flowing movements with a total physical experience. Rhythmic gymnasts perform four sequences of movements to music. In each sequence they move with a different piece of apparatus: the ball, the ribbon, clubs, the hoop or the rope. The apparatus is not a decoration, but must be constantly moving; it should appear to be part of the body and the body movement. Six judges score each performance out of ten.

Rhythmic gymnastics first became an Olympic event for women in 1984.

Canadian Sport Images, F. Scott Grant

Lisa Simes shows the grace and beauty that has made Olympic gymnastics such a popular event with spectators, even those who do not generally watch sports.

The Olympics have become such a big event that athletes sometimes see the Games as their one and only chance to make it big, and will perform even when seriously injured. This is called playing through pain. Shun Fujimoto of Japan showed the world the meaning of courage and loyalty at the 1976 Montreal Olympics. He broke his leg during the floor exercises routine. Refusing to let his teammates down, he did not tell his coaches or teammates about the extent of his injury, and performed on the pommel horse and rings.

Amazingly he scored 9.5 on the horse and 9.7 on the rings. As he dismounted from the rings, the brave Fujimoto had to land on both feet. When he did, he dislocated his knee as well. Grimacing in pain with a broken leg and dislocated knee, Fujimoto could not hide his tears. He could go on no further but he did not let his team down. His points helped Japan (576.85) edge the Soviet Union (576.45) for the men's team gymnastics gold medal.

Men's Olympics gymnastics, shown here from Montreal in 1976, is more a test of strength.

Team Sports

Team sports are an exciting part of Olympic competition. There were, however, no team games in the first modern Olympic Games in Athens in 1896. Water polo was added as the first team sport in the 1900 Olympic Games in Paris. Unofficial soccer (football) matches were played in the 1900 and 1904 Games. In 1908 it became an official Olympic sport. Field hockey was also added in 1908. Since then basketball, handball, volleyball and baseball have been added as Olympic sports.

Tennis action from the 1924 Paris Olympics. Do women still wear dresses and skirts when playing? Hardly.

Tennis for men was one of the sports in the first Olympic Games, but was dropped in 1924. It reappeared at the Seoul Games in 1988.

Very few people have ever had a vacation like the one John Pius Boland enjoyed in 1896. He was a student at Oxford University and learned about the rebirth of the Olympic Games that year in Athens. So he decided to take a holiday to see it. The British team at Athens had only six athlete on it, and so the tourist Boland picked up a tennis racquet and entered the Games competition on the spur of the moment. The officials said sure. The Games were not as structured as they are now.

The tourist ended up winning the gold medal in men's singles and doubles. How about that for your next holiday? Just tell your parents you want to go on vacation and that you want to come home with two Olympic gold medals as souvenirs. Hey, it beats Mickey Mouse ears from Disneyland.

Success in water polo requires all thirteen players on a team to be great swimmers, accurate left- and right-handed throwers and catchers, and tough competitors. Only the goalkeeper is allowed to touch the bottom of the pool.

Sportsmanship is important, whether you're playing Little League baseball, basketball or netball for your school team, or just road hockey, street cricket or touch football with your friends. But one men's field hockey team did not display good sportsmanship at the 1972 Munich Summer Olympics. After it lost 1-0 in the gold medal game because of what they thought was poor officiating, the players shoved the referee, hit a Games doctor and poured water on another official. During the medal ceremonies, the players laughed and joked and refused to stand at attention. The eleven players were banned for life from the Olympics for their behavior but were allowed back in for the next Games in Montreal in 1976.

In addition to volleyball, three other net-type games played by individuals or partners are official Olympic sports: tennis, table tennis and badminton.

Women's teams were not included in Olympic competition until 1964, when a women's volleyball competition was held. Now they also compete in basketball, handball, field hockey and the other net sports. Beach volleyball, women's soccer and women's softball will join the Olympic roster at the 1996 Atlanta Summer Olympics.

The Japanese women's volleyball team (in blue) has won two gold medals, two silvers and a bronze since the sport was introduced into the Olympics in 1964 at Tokyo.

The British taught India field hockey but soon the students became the masters. India won Olympic gold in men's field hockey six straight times from 1928 in Amsterdam to 1956 in Melbourne and again in 1964 at Tokyo and 1980 at Moscow. That's eight golds. Wow! India also won silver in 1960 and bronzes in 1968 and 1972.

Soccer is called football everywhere in the world except North America and Australia.

Dead Heads at the Olympics? Yes. The famous rock and roll band, the Grateful Dead, sponsored the Lithuanian men's basketball team at the 1992 Barcelona Summer Olympics. The Lithuanians had a good team but not a lot of money. The Grateful Dead heard about this and decided to help. Lithuania beat Russia for the bronze medal. During the medals ceremony, the Lithuanian players wore tie-dyed 1960s T-shirts the Dead had donated to the team.

NBA stars Sir Charles Barkley (left) and the Admiral, David Robinson, in action with the U.S. basketball team at the 1992 Barcelona Olympics.

Some great basketball superstars have played in the Olympic Games — Michael Jordan, Magic Johnson, Larry Bird, Charles Barkley, David Robinson, Patrick Ewing, Spencer Haywood, Jerry West, Oscar Robertson and Bill Russell. But the first Olympic basketball tournament was held on some old outdoor clay tennis courts surrounded by about two thousand temporary bleachers at the 1936 Berlin Games and was a long way away from the Dream Team and the 1992 Barcelona Games.

Canadian-born James Naismith, the inventor of the game, was hardly accorded the hero's welcome one might have expected. He was invited as a guest of honor but when he got to the Olympics, there weren't even any tickets waiting for him. The American team arranged passes for him to attend the games and drummed up a quick parade and party in his honor at the Athletes Village. Only about 200 people bothered to attend the Naismith functions.

It rained heavily both the night before and the day of the gold medal final between the U.S. and Canada. The rain turned the clay courts into a mud bath. The ball wouldn't bounce. It was as if horses had ploughed up the floor before the game. The awful conditions didn't allow anything resembling basketball to be played. The U.S. led 15-4 at halftime in the bizarre game, as players slipped and slid all over the court and the sopping wet ball squirted every which way. The players couldn't make sharp cuts or dribble the ball. The teams scored just four points each in the second half as the U.S. won the gold medal with a 19-8 victory.

Adding to the weirdness of this first Olympic gold medal final were the American's uniforms and shorts. They had to borrow things from other teams after the U.S. locker room was robbed during the team's final round-robin game. But that gold-medal victory over Canada represented the fourth contest in what became a 62-game U.S. winning streak in Olympic men's basketball, stretching all the way to 1972 and the controversial loss in the final at Munich.

The United States won 62 straight men's Olympic basketball games and seven consecutive gold medals until it all came to a wild end at Munich in 1972. Doug Collins of the U.S. scored two free throws with three seconds remaining to give the Americans a 50-49 lead — their first of the final game against the Soviets. The U.S. streak looked as if it would continue.

The game ended twice with the Americans mobbing themselves on the court each time. But the clock was set back to three seconds in a controversial administrative move. The Soviets lobbed the ball down court. It was caught by a big man named Sasha Belov, who calmly put it in the basket at the buzzer. This time it was the Soviets' turn to mob themselves on the floor as the dejected Americans watched in anger and disbelief. The Americans refused to accept their silver medals and boycotted the medal ceremonies. Those medals remain in a vault at the IOC headquarters in Switzerland. Each member of that 1972 U.S. team has made a vow to never go there and pick up his medal.

Cycling

Bicycle racing can be divided into three types: road racing, track racing and mountain biking. Olympic road races take place outdoors over long, often brutal courses. Strength and endurance of almost heroic proportions are necessary to win some of these races. Competitors for the individual road race begin from a massed start and race approximately 200 km over a prescribed course.

In Olympic team trials, each team of four races the clock on the course. The times of the fastest three tream members are used to determine the winners. Switching the lead and providing a slipstream for other team members is an important strategy.

Track races are shorter and take place in a velodrome. In track racing it is necessary not only to outlast your opponents, but to outwit them. Track racers participate in sprints, with two or three racers at a time; in time trials, with cyclists taking turns to race 1 km against the clock; in individual pursuit races in which racers start at opposite sides of the track and try to overtake each other; and in team pursuit races, where teams of four riders pursue each other around the track.

Mountain biking makes its Olympic debut at Atlanta in 1996.

Canadian Sport Images, F. Scott Grant

Have you ever had trouble deciding what to do? It happens to everybody. Sometimes it's hard to make up your mind. Russell Mockridge of Australia didn't know what he wanted his job to be. He was an excellent bike rider but he wanted to do other things, too. He became a newspaper writer and then studied to become an artist so he could draw good pictures. Then he decided to become a minister. But everybody kept telling him: "Russell, keep riding your bike…keep riding your bike. You are very good at it." So Russell did. He kept riding his bike. He kept riding it until he won two gold medals at the 1952 Helsinki Olympics.

Olympic cyclists have been known to reach speeds of 70 kph. That's nearly as fast as a car on the freeway!

Combatives

Now don't confuse Olympic wrestling with the WWF. There are no masked villains with capes. Olympic wrestling is a real and honest sport. Greco-Roman wrestling has been in the Olympics since 1896 and freestyle joined the agenda in 1904. What's the difference? Greco-Roman prohibits any holds below the waist. Freestyle allows holds above and below the waist. They require different tactics in order to win. Among the interesting rules is that wrestlers must be clean shaven or have a well-grown beard. Why? Because a stubble beard can cause great irritation on an opponent's skin!

Three knockdowns in one round or four in one bout end the match in Olympic boxing.

Combat between two athletes features skill, strategy and suspense.

Don't confuse Olympic **boxing** with the professional sport. The rules are quite different. Rules in Olympic boxing protect the safety of boxers. Olympic boxers, who must be seventeen years old, box for three, three-minute rounds and get points for hitting their opponents in specific target areas. Contestants are awarded points for the accuracy of their punches. Amateur boxers compete in twelve weight classes.

Fencers compete with three different weapons: the foil, the epee (or dueling sword) and the saber. In all three events, touches with sword tip on the opponent's torso or target area are scored as points. The target area includes all the vital organs. Today the touches are recorded electronically. Modern Olympic fencers wear special suits which are attached to electronic sensors which record a touch. Hits on the target area are indicated by a system of lights.

Judo means "to do things the gentle way," and combines a military art from Japan with a disciplined development of spiritual and physical fitness. One of the mottoes of judo is "strong within, but gentle without." Participants go barefoot on a mat and wear a traditional white Japanese tunic and pants outfit called a *judogi*. Swift, clever movement — not violence — is the key to overcoming an opponent. The primary aim is to end the contest by executing a clean throw and scoring an *ippon*. However, points can also be obtained by controlling the opponent in hold downs. A judo match lasts until one fighter has scored one full *ippon* or until the end of allotted time. The result after allotted time is determined by minor points scored and penalties incurred.

Taekwondo is a Korean military art in which participants use only their hands and feet in simulated movements which would stun or kill an enemy. It was first introduced as a demonstration sport in the Olympic Games in Seoul in 1988.

Olympic **weightlifting** involves two events for participants in a variety of weight categories. The "snatch" requires a violent, explosive lift. The lifter brings the bar from the floor to an overhead position in one movement. While bending his legs in a squat or split position, he then stands up straight, holding the bar motionless on fully extended arms.

The "clean and jerk" is a two-part lift. The lifter first brings the barbell from the ground to shoulder height while he splits or bends his legs. Then he jerks the bar above his head and finishes by standing up with legs braced and arms extended. Three referees judge the validity of the lifts.

Olympic **wrestling** is a completely different sport from professional wrestling. The object of wrestling is to demonstrate control of the opponent by placing him on his back and pinning his two shoulders on the mat for one second. A pin brings immediate victory. Other holds earn points according to a fixed scale. The accumulated total points determines the winner at the end of the bout.

The great Soviet weightlifter Vasiley Alexeev won two Olympic gold medals in 1972 and 1976 and was the world's strongest man. For breakfast alone, he used to eat a 42-egg omelet, several pints of milk and 20 pieces of toast. For lunch he would gobble down eight steaks and drink 20 pints of beer. You probably don't each that much in a single month! But Alexeev never became a movie star like the silver medalist in the light-heavyweight class of the 1948 London Olympics — Harold Sakata, who went on to play Oddjob in the James Bond movie Goldfinger.

Men have always liked to challenge each other one-on-one in combat sports like boxing, judo and wrestling. There are paintings 5,000 years old on cave walls depicting men wrestling. Combat is as old as humankind itself.

Those ancestors of ours who drew those cave pictures could not have possibly imagined Cassius Clay, who was a lively and very talkative eighteen-year-old boxer at the 1960 Rome Olympics. Everywhere he went in the Athletes Village, he would stop people and talk to them and get his picture taken with them. And he would tell everybody how he was going to win the light-heavyweight gold medal. He did that. He loved his gold medal.

When he got home to Louisville in the United States, he ate supper with it around his neck and even slept with it on. He wore it so much that the gold began to wear off. On the way home after meeting the mayor, Cassius stopped at a restaurant for a hamburger and milkshake. The waitress would not serve him because he was black and the restaurant was for white people only. That was the law back then in the southern United States. That law was wrong and Cassius hated that law. Cassius showed the waitress his gold medal but she still said no.

Later that day, some white boys wanted to beat up Cassius. That was a mistake. He didn't want to fight nor did he start the fight. But he ended it by beating them up, instead. At the end of this horrible day, Cassius felt so bad about all the things that had happened in the restaurant and in the fight. He went to the top of a bridge and threw his gold medal into the Ohio River. Although he threw away his beloved Olympic medal in anger and disgust, Cassius didn't throw away his talent. He became Muhammad Ali, one of the greatest professional boxers of all-time.

The sport of wrestling is one of the most venerable in the Olympic Games. It is certainly the oldest. It goes back 5,000 years, and some of the holds you see today on the Olympic mats were used by the ancient peoples of Greece and Egypt thousands of years ago. Wrestling has been an Olympic sport since the first modern Games in 1896 at Athens. That's about as Olympic as you can get.

Equestrian

Equestrian events feature two superb athletes: the rider and the horse. To be successful, both must be in top shape and communicate successfully through a subtle set of hand and knee pressure signals. Equestrian athletes compete in three different sports: dressage, show jumping and the three-day event.

In dressage, competitors perform a series of required gaits, pirouettes and changes of direction within a set period of time. These exercises demonstrate the harmonious development of a horse's physique and ability, requiring it to be supple, calm, confident, attentive and keen and to achieve perfect understanding with its rider. The horse is thus able to give the impression that it is doing on its own what the rider requires.

Show jumping courses are designed to rigid specifications and test the horse and rider's ability to negotiate a variety of fences of various heights, widths and combinations. Points are deducted for faults (obstacles knocked down, failure to clear a jump, disobedience, refusal to jump, etc.). In addition, time faults are given for exceeding the time allowed. An Olympic team jumping competition involves four riders, each participating in two rounds of jumping.

The three-day event is usually the first on the equestrian Olympic program and is an exhausting competition. It features a dressage test, a demanding, four-phase endurance day, and a stadium jumping competition.

On the first day of the three-day event, horses and riders participate in the dressage test. The endurance day, Day 2, begins with a 16–20 km streets and roads "warm-up" at a speed of 240 m per minute. Next, in phase B, they jump

Mark Todd and his great horse Charisma of New Zealand were one of the great horse and rider combinations of all time and won gold in the individual three-day event at the 1984 Los Angeles and 1988 Seoul Olympics. But did you know Todd had no money to get to the Games? He was a dairy farmer and had to sell most of his cows in order to get the money to train for the Olympics. His determination paid off with two gold medals.

It was like-father-like-son for the Roycroft family of Australia. Bill Roycroft and his son Wayne won the bronze medal in the three-day equestrian team event at the 1968 Mexico City Olympics. And then they did the same thing again at the 1976 Montreal Olympics. One family, two bronze medals. And Bill Roycroft was sixty-one years old — old enough to be a grandfather — when he and Wayne won their second medal in 1976. You may not be able to run or swim in the Games when you're that old, but you can certainly ride a horse.

Equestrian and shooting are the only two sports in the Olympics where men and women compete directly against each other.

It is odd that such a formerly stodgy sport should now be so progressive. Before the 1952 Helsinki Olympics, only commissioned officers in the army were allowed to compete in the individual dressage event. How fair was that? In 1952 the rules were changed and anybody was allowed to enter.

Lis Hartel, a housewife from Denmark, was one of those people. She got polio when she was twenty-two years old and couldn't walk. She had to crawl around. She got a little better but still could not use any muscles beneath her knees. She had no feeling in her feet. You could step on her toes and she couldn't feel it. But she could ride! She had to be helped on and off her horse, Jubilee. But that didn't stop Hartel from winning the silver medal at both the 1952 and 1956 Olympics behind Henri St. Cyr of Sweden. Hartel deserved a gold medal, however, for determination.

several large brush fences at a very fast pace. Then they "cool down" on a lengthy trot down the roads and tracks, and are examined by a vet for their fitness to proceed to the cross-country phase.

In the cross-country phase, the already-tired horses and riders, gallop another 8 km over every imaginable type of terrain. There must be at least twenty-five ditches, banks, drops, water jumps and combination jumps. The horse, which has never seen the course, must be superbly conditioned. The rider, who has walked the course, needs courage and know-how to guide a trusting, galloping horse over these difficult and often unusual obstacles.

On Day 3, horses and riders who remain in the competition compete in the stadium jumping competition. Then all penalties from all phases of the three-day event are totalled and the horse and rider with the lowest score win the medal.

Boating

Wherever people build boats, people race boats. Three kinds of boats are used in Olympic competitions: boats with paddles (canoes/kayaks), boats with oars (rowboats) and boats with sails (yachts).

Canoeing events involve two kinds of boats: kayaks with enclosed decks and canoes with open decks. In the kayak or K-boat class, paddlers sit in the boat with knees slightly raised and feet on a rudder used to steer the boat. Kayakers paddle with a double-ended paddle. In the Canadian canoe or C-boat class, paddlers kneel on one knee and paddle with a single paddle. They steer by using different strokes of their paddles. Kayak events involve one, two or four paddlers. Canoe events involve one or two paddlers.

Olympic rowers participate in sculling or rowing events. The rower has one oar; the sculler has two sculls or short, light oars. There are events for singles, doubles, fours and eights.

Canadian Sport Images

One of the most bizarre moments in Olympic boating history came on the dock at the 1956 Melbourne Games. After being presented with the single sculls rowing gold medal, Vyacheslav Ivanov of the Soviet Union was so happy that he leaped off the podium. But he landed so hard that he dropped his medal and it rolled off the dock and into the lake. He madly dived in after it but couldn't find it because the lake was too deep. The International Olympic Committee felt sorry for Ivanov and gave him a replacement medal. Decades later, an Australian diver found the lost 1956 gold medal sitting at the bottom of Lake Wendouree.

Larry Lemieux of Canada didn't win a medal in Finn-class yachting at the 1988 Seoul Olympics but he won a lot more. He won the admiration of the world. He was in second place in the fifth race of the Olympic competition when he saw a Singapore boat had flipped over in the rough waters and the competitor was in the water and in danger of drowning because he was hurt and unable to swim in the tough currents. Not caring about his race, Lemieux turned around and saved Joseph Chan. Lemieux showed the true spirit of the Olympic Games and was given a special trophy by the International Olympic Committee.

As this competitor from the 1972 Munich Games shows, kayak slalom singles (also known as whitewater canoeing) is one of the most hazardous Olympic events, as the kayakers paddle up and down an obstacle course. But it sort of looks like fun, doesn't it? Something like a ride at Disney World.

The yacht was a spiffy little sailing invention of the 1400s, designed originally to fight pirates. From these hit-and-run vessels evolved the small boats used for pleasure and then racing. Yachts harness the power of the wind by using sails which are handled by a crew. Sails act like the wings of an airplane, lifting the boat forward.

There are ten classes of yachts in Olympic competition.

- The Solings and Stars have weighted keels for stability.
- The 470s, Flying Dutchmans and Finns have a centerboard and rely primarily on moving the crew around for stability.
- The Tornado catamarans are twin-hull boats, built for speed.
- Sailboarding was introduced as an Olympic event in 1984.
- Laser becomes at Olympic event at Atlanta in 1996.

Races sailed on the Olympic course are expected to take about three hours. They are started by an anchored committee boat firing a warning gun and hoisting a white flag ten minutes before the start. Five minutes later, another shot is fired and a blue flag is hoisted. Officially, the race is on when the last shot is fired and a red flag is hoisted.

There are seven races in each class, and each yacht counts the best six results for a total score.

Henry Pearce of Australia proved at the 1928 Amsterdam Olympics that nice guys do finish first. When a family of ducks paddled single file in front of Pearce's boat in the single sculls rowing final, Pearce stopped and let them pass rather than row over them and likely kill them. He still won the gold medal by five lengths. He won another gold medal four years later at Los Angeles. But no ducks got in his way there.

Modern Pentathlon

In the early years of the modern Olympic Games, Pierre de Coubertin, dreamed up a sport which would highlight the true all-round athlete — one who could excel in all of the military and gentlemanly sports. He talked the Swedes into organizing the sport for their Olympic Games in 1912.

Athletes in modern pentathlon compete over five days in equestrian, fencing, shooting, swimming and running events. Each competitor begins with a base score of 1000 points for each event. Points are added for achievement and deducted for faults.

The fifth place finisher in the modern pentathlon at the 1912 Stockholm Olympics was a twenty-six-year-old American named George S. Patton. He later became one of the most famous generals in World War II. He was so famous that a movie was made about him. Patton *was named the Academy Award winner as the best film of 1970 and George C. Scott won the Oscar as best actor for playing the part of Patton in the movie. But as great a general as Patton became, he lost the gold medal at the 1912 Olympics because he couldn't shoot straight. That's right — the great general couldn't shoot straight! He placed only twenty-first in the shooting part of the modern pentathlon. Had he done well in that portion of the event, he would have won the gold medal.*

The Swedes organized the first competition in modern pentathlon so well they won most of the medals in the sport for the next thirty years.

Most modern pentathlon medals are won by military men.

Fencing is just one of the five very different sports that an Olympic modern pentathlete must be good at.

Target Sports

It's white-dress-only in archery, which first came into the Olympics in 1972 at Munich.

Women competed in the archery events in 1904 and 1908.

Archery and shooting are the two target sports of the Olympic Games. Both activities began with far more serious objectives than winning medals — hunting and warfare. In both, technology became the means whereby human beings could dominate their environment. With the advent of gun powder, the bow and arrow was replaced by the firearm. Archery continued its popularity, however, as a sport for both men and women.

Target archery was included in the Olympic Games of 1900, 1904, 1908 and 1920 but was dropped again until 1972. The archery competition involves a series of elimination rounds. Men shoot 36 arrows each from 90 m, 70 m, 50 m and 30 m distance. Women shoot from 70 m, 60 m, 50 m and 30 m. Targets for the 50 m and 30 m rounds are smaller. In the first elimination, the top 24 competitors begin a new round, then the top 18, then the top 12, then the top 8.

There are two types of events in the sport of Olympic shooting. In the one group of events, shooters aim at targets, and various types of rifles and pistols are used. Shooters fire from different positions — prone, kneeling and standing — at paper targets with circular scoring rings.

In the second type of shooting event, shooters fire at clay saucers which fly up like birds. In fact, in the early Games the targets were live pigeons. The usual firearm is a 12-gauge double-barreled shot gun. In skeet shooting the shooter tries to hit two targets released together. The first target is like a grouse taking flight, and the second like a bird flying quickly overhead.

In trap shooting shooters try to nail a target released on command, which whizes away in unpredictable directions. They are allowed two shots at the same target — on from each barrel of their shotgun. Both trap and skeet events involve rounds of twenty-five targets each.

Charlotte Dod, who was thirty-six when she won a silver medal in archery in 1908, was one of the world's great athletes. She had already won the Wimbledon tennis competition five times, the British ladies golf title, and played on the English women's field hockey team.

Gilmour Boa's unselfishness helped a fellow-Canadian earn a gold medal at the 1956 Melbourne Olympics. Gerry Ouellette did not shoot well in his first event. So Boa lent Ouellette his rifle for the prone part of the smallbore rifle event, even though it meant that Boa himself would have to hurry his shots in order to let Ouellette also have the rifle. Boa won the bronze medal for Canada. But on the top podium with the gold medal was Ouellette — with Boa's rifle! Ouellette gave Canada a gold medal with a perfect score of 600. But that world mark was later thrown out of the record books because the Melbourne Games organizers had accidentally placed the target about two metres too close. But Ouellette got to keep his gold medal.

Ouellette switched rifles but at least he didn't have to switch hands like Karoly Takacs of Hungary in the rapid fire pistol shooting event at the 1948 London Olympics. During World War II, a grenade exploded in Takacs' hand. His right hand — his shooting hand — was blown right off. After the war, he learned to shoot with his left hand. And he won an Olympic gold medal.

Sports of the Olympic Winter Games

Canadian Sport Images, Claus Andersen

Skier Kate Pace of Canada shows her form at the 1994 Lillehammer Winter Olympics.

Every four years the Winter Olympic Games celebrate sports that take place on ice and snow. They now take place two years after the summer Games.

ALPINE SKIING

A green light flashes, a barrier opens, a body in yellow hurtles down a steep, icy and dangerous slope. Racing against the clock, he digs his edges into the curves and crouches over his skis on the straight-aways. He flies over the bumps, heading for the finish line. This is Olympic alpine skiing. By the time the Olympics are over an alpine skier may have competed in all four of the Olympic skiing events: the downhill race, a slalom race which zigzags through a series of flags or gates, a giant slalom and a super giant slalom. All of these events are based on the challenge of getting from the top to the bottom of a snow-covered mountain on skis in the fastest possible time. Only hundredths of a second separate winners from losers.

CROSS-COUNTRY SKIING

For the tenth time in this race Andrea strides powerfully on her skis up the big hill, planting her ski poles purposefully as she goes. From the edge of the course, her coach calls out her time. She is a few seconds in the lead. "Keep up the pace," he encourages.

Olympic cross-country skiers race on a prepared course that has equal portions of uphill, downhill and level ground. They participate in 15, 30 and 50 km races for men and 5, 10 and 20 km races for women, and also in relays.

SKI JUMPING

From the top of the 90 m Olympic ski jump the ground is a long way down. And from down below, the skier who is sitting on the "in-run" waiting for the "go" light looks very small. At the signal, he starts his jump by skiing down the in-run getting as much speed as he can. As he flies off the jump, he stretches his body out over his skis to reduce wind resistance, lands with his knees bent and one foot in front of the other.

Great landing; good distance! He slows himself down on the out-run, waves to the thousands of people who are watching and looks back to check his scores. This is Olympic ski jumping.

BIATHLON

With nerves of steel Marion calms down, slows down her breathing and aims her rifle at the black and white target 50 m in front of her. She shoots and a white lid flops down over the target. Good shot! She fires four more times, hits every shot, slings her rifle back over her shoulder and races out of the target range and back onto the cross-country course for another 5 km run.

A happy skier at the 1992 Albertville Winter Olympics.

A poster from the 1984 Sarajevo Winter Olympics.

A historic shot of speed skating action from the 1932 Lake Placid Winter Olympics.

In biathlon, athletes combine the endurance of cross-country skiing with the precision and skill of .22 calibre rifle shooting. They ski a total of 20 km in five laps. After each lap, they return to the range to shoot — twice from a standing position and twice lying down.

FIGURE SKATING

On the ice a young couple in brilliant purple costumes end their long program with a series of spins and a death spiral. Their Olympic competition is now over. Breathing heavily from the exertion of their four-minute performance, they wait for the judges scores. Will they win that Olympic medal that they have worked for for so many years?

Olympic figure skaters combine grace and drama with great courage and athletic ability. They compete in singles events for men and women, pairs events which feature jumps, lifts and spins, and ice dancing which features creative and synchronized footwork in time to prescribed musical rhythms. A panel of judges scores each performance on a scale from 0 to 6.

SPEED SKATING

Rene is an Olympic speed skating champion. When he is racing at top speed he travels faster over the ice on his long blades than any human being without mechanical assistance, reaching speeds of more than 50 kph. In Olympic speed skating men and women compete in 500 m, 1000 m, 1500 m and 5000 m races.

Men also compete in a 10,000 m race and women in a 3000 m race. Most competitive speed-skating tracks are now in indoor arenas. The skaters race in a counterclockwise direction, changing lanes with each lap. Races are run in pairs, against time.

ICE HOCKEY

"He shoots; he scores," echoes around the walls of the Olympic hockey arena. Fast-paced Olympic hockey is played on a larger ice surface than NHL hockey, and there are rules which control violence and fighting. Otherwise, the two games are the same, with five skaters plus goalie per team on the ice, and with frequent line changes.

Olympic hockey players are superb skaters, skilled puck handlers and skilled strategists. Hockey is the only team sport in the Olympic Winter Games. Getting the puck in the net is the objective.

BOBSLED

The only thing separating you and your partner from the ice-encrusted track is a thin fiberglass cocoon on runners. Before you is an icy tunnel, open to the sky. Ahead is a curve to the left, then another to the right. You move instinctively with your sled. Fight it! Don't black out! You've never taken this S-curve at this speed. Don't panic. You're going to win it here, boys.

The Olympic rings form a shadow on the ice while the hockey team practises during the 1960 Winter Games in Squaw Valley, California.

A poster for the 1980 Winter Olympics in Lake Placid, New York.

Bobsled is a dangerous sport. Two-man and four-man sleds reach speeds up to 150 kph from a standing start. It takes approximately one minute for Olympic bobsledders to make a descent on a bob run. On the tighter corners of the track, riders are subjected to G-forces of up to four and a half times the weight of gravity. Success on the track depends on the mechanical perfection of the sled, the initial thrust given by the entire crew at the start and the expertise of the driver on the way down.

LUGE

In North America on snowy days, suitable hills are besieged by children with toboggans. In the European mountains, where the snow is much wetter, these same kids would use a wooden sleigh on runners. In French this sleigh is called a *luge*.

Olympic lugers lie on their backs on a small flat sled to race down tunnels of solid ice. Although they sometimes reach speeds of 150 kph there is no braking device. As a general rule, competitors want to remain flat and motionless, in a balanced, neutral position. They steer by subtly shifting their body weight. There are three luge events in Olympic competition: men's and women's singles and men's doubles.

The Winter Olympics have thrice been held in the United States and on two of these occasions, the Americans managed to unexpectedly win the ice hockey gold medal with dramatic flair. The Americans were not highly regarded when they entered the 1960 Winter Games in Squaw Valley, California. They had lost to university and minor league teams on the way to Squaw Valley.

But then something magical happened for the Americans. They won all seven of their Games at the Olympics to claim the gold medal. A key moment was the 2-1 victory over Canada. Another big American win was a 3-2 victory over the defending gold medalists from the Soviet Union. It was the first time the U.S. had ever beaten the Soviets in ice hockey.

The U.S. players were exhausted in their seventh and final game and looked as if they couldn't skate another shift. Czechoslovakia led 4-3 after two periods and the Americans' golden dream seemed over. But then the Soviet captain burst into the U.S. dressing room during the intermission. Speaking no English, Nikolai Sologubov put his hand over his mouth. That meant the American players should take some oxygen. They got a tank of it and then felt much better. The Cold War between the Americans and Soviets had melted for a bit — at the Winter Games of all places — with that very sportsmanlike gesture. The Americans felt so good after that hit of oxygen they scored six goals in the third period to win the game 9-4 and the gold medal.

Then came the Miracle on Ice at the 1980 Winter Olympics in Lake Placid, New York. Ice hockey is Canada's passion and in many ways it defines that country of ice and snow. Canada won every Olympic gold medal in ice hockey between 1920 and 1952 except one, when it took the silver medal behind Britain in 1936 at Garmisch-Partenkirchen, Germany. But the British team did it with twelve Canadians on its roster! In all, Canada won six of the first seven Olympic gold medals presented in ice hockey.

The Soviet Union, like Canada, is a cold country and its sports leaders thought ice hockey was a sport that perfectly suited their nation. So they learned the game from old Canadian film reels and started to dominate at the Olympics. Between 1956 and 1988, the Soviets won seven of the nine Olympic gold medals awarded in ice hockey. The only two times they didn't, the underdog Americans did.

The second time was the Miracle on Ice at Lake Placid in 1980, when a rag-tag group of Americans, who were only ranked seventh of the 12 teams entered, pulled off one of the most stunning upsets in Olympic history. The Americans played by the seat of their pants in their round-robin contests and won and tied some key games with late goals and managed to squeeze into the medal round of four teams, where they first faced the Soviet Union.

The Soviets boasted the best goalie in the world, Vladislav Tretiak, and a virtual galaxy of world stars up front like Vyacheslav Fetisov, Vladimir Krutov, Alexandr Maltsev, Boris Mikhailov, Vladimir Petrov, Valery Kharlamov, Helmut Balderis and Sergei Makarov. It was a true Dream Team of hockey. But the Americans beat the Soviets 4-3 in a real shocker and then held off Finland 4-2 for the gold medal.

The Record Book

MOST GOLD MEDALS (CAREER)

No, it's not Carl Lewis. The record for the most career Olympic gold medals goes to American Ray Ewry. Ray Who? you might ask. Ewry won his 10 gold medals between 1900 and 1908 in the standing high, long and triple jump events. Those events are no longer contested. Ewry was paralyzed as a boy but overcame that through his dedication to sports. His strong legs came about because he exercised so long and so hard to overcome not being able to walk as a child.

MOST GOLD MEDALS (SINGLE OLYMPICS)

Do you think anybody will ever break American swimmer Mark Spitz's record of seven gold medals, set at the Munich Games in 1972? After he accomplished that great feat, he was immediately taken out of Munich and sent home because he felt his life may have been been in danger. Spitz is Jewish and eleven Jewish athletes had been killed at the Munich Olympics.

His record will probably stand for a long time. And Spitz is glad it will. He had predicted he would win six gold medals at the 1968 Mexico City Olympics and looked sheepish when he only won two, both in the relays. Is it wise to brag like that? It's probably not a good idea to be too boastful. Spitz's lesson from the 1968 Olympics is a good one for everybody to learn. But so is the lesson of his hard work and his refusal to quit. Look what happened in Munich because he wouldn't give up!

Handsome American swim hero Mark Spitz shows off the record seven gold medals he won at the 1972 Munich Summer Olympics.

MOST MEDALS

Two Russians gymnasts hold the Olympic records for the most medals won in a career and also in a single Games. Larissa Latynina competed in the 1956 Melbourne, 1960 Rome and 1964 Tokyo Olympics for the Soviet Union and won 18 medals, nine of them gold. Wow! She has enough to open her own jewelry store.

And move over Mark Spitz. They weren't all gold, but Alexandr Ditiatin won eight medals at the 1980 Moscow Olympics. He could open a jewelry store, too.

OLDEST GOLD MEDALIST

Oscar Swahn was 64 years and 258 days old when he won the running deer shooting event at the 1912 Stockholm Olympics. That is old enough to be your grandfather! Swahn also holds the Olympic record as the oldest competitor. He was 72 years and 280 days old when he competed in the 1920 Antwerp Games. That's old enough to be your great-grandfather!

YOUNGEST GOLD MEDALLIST

The Dutch crew in the pair-oared rowing event in the 1900 Paris Olympics decided that their coxswain was too heavy. So they replaced him in the final with a little French boy who was watching the races on the shores of the river. The boy's name is not known. But he was not more than ten years old and some think as young as seven. This small French boy is the youngest person ever to win an Olympic gold medal. But still nobody knows his name.

In the Olympics, there are no second chances. If you don't show up for your race on time, you are disqualified.

Eddie Hart and Rey Robinson of the U.S. were serious threats for gold in the men's 100 metres at the 1972 Munich Olympics. But they were told by their coach Stan Wright that their quarterfinal races were just after 6 P.M. on August 31. So Hart and Robinson made their way to the stadium at 4 P.M. On the way, they stopped into the broadcast center to say hello to some friends.

Robinson saw on the TV screens that men were warming up for a 100 m race and asked if it was a replay of the morning heats. He was informed that no, it was a live feed from the stadium. They were watching the warm up for THEIR event! Their coach had misread 16:15 on the schedule as 6:15 P.M. (16:15 is the international way of writing 4:15 P.M.) The panicked sprinters got into a car and raced to the stadium, but they were too late. Their races had already been run by the time they got there.

Tug-o-war action from the 1920 Antwerp Summer Olympics. This is just one of many unusual and strange sporting events that were once part of the Olympics but are no longer contested. Some others include: croquet, lacrosse, motor boating, polo, rugby and rackets.

The standing long jump event at the 1904 St. Louis Olympics.

FIRST TELEVISED OLYMPICS

The Olympics are now seen by billions of people on television around the world. In fact, 99.99 percent of the people who watch the Games do so on television and not by actually travelling to the host city to watch in person. You will probably watch the Olympics on TV, too. The first use of television at the Olympics happened during the 1936 Berlin Games. The muddy and ghostly images were beamed from some Games venues to eighteen television halls around Berlin and the Athletes Village. A few thousand very confused people gathered to watch and gaze at what we all take for granted today.

"The TV at the Village provided a very fuzzy image," recalls Doug Peden, a basketball player for Canada at the Berlin Games. "But I recognized Syl Apps [a Canadian pole vaulter] warming up at the stadium. And here I was miles away from the stadium. It's hard to comprehend now what a thing this was to experience. It was very crude, but to us it was amazing. We didn't even know they were working on that stuff. I didn't even have an inkling about the concept of the thing [television]." Now it seems we live in front of the television.

TALLEST OLYMPIAN

The tallest player in the Olympics was probably seven-foot-three Russian basketball player Yanis Kruminsch at the 1960 Rome Games. That's the size of a small tree! But as tall as Kruminsch was, it didn't help the Soviet Union win a gold medal. They took silver behind the United States team, which included future NBA stars Oscar Robertson, Jerry West and Jerry Lucas. And nothing happened to Kruminsch like what happened to seven-foot American basketball player Bob Kurland at the 1948 London Olympics. A Chinese player dribbled between the legs of the tall Kurland and scored a basket!

SMALLEST OLYMPIAN

Figure skater Sonja Henie of Norway was only four-foot-three-inches tall and weighed a mere sixty pounds when she finished eighth in the 1924 Winter Olympics in Chamonix, France, and is probably the smallest Olympian. She went on to win the women's singles figure-skating gold medal at the 1928, 1932 and 1936 Winter Olympics. As a grown woman, she grew to only five feet and weighed only 100 pounds. Did you know Henie's father owned the first automobile in Oslo and that she became a famous Hollywood movie actress?

The smallest male Olympian may have been Joe De Pietro, who won gold for the U.S. in the bantamweight weightlifting division at the 1948 London Summer Olympics despite being only four-foot-six-inches tall. That's the size of someone in elementary school! He was truly Little Joe.

HEAVIEST OLYMPIAN

That just may have been weightlifter Humberto Selvetti of Argentina, who tipped the scales at 316 pounds at the 1956 Melbourne Summer Olympics. Lucky he didn't break the scales. Selvetti and American Paul Anderson lifted the same amount in the heavyweight class and tied for first place. But Anderson, not exactly slim himself at 304 pounds, was given the Olympic gold medal because he weighed 12 pounds less than Selvetti.

Maybe Selvetti should have gone on a diet.

The smallest Olympian ever was the great Sonja Henie of Norway.

Issues in the Olympic Family

BOYCOTTS

In modern times, countries have sometimes used the Olympics for political purposes, most often to show that they are not happy about what another country is doing. They do this by means of a boycott, which means to refuse to attend.

A total of twenty-two countries, mostly from Africa, boycotted the 1976 Montreal Olympics to protest New Zealand being there. The New Zealand rugby team had played South Africa, a country which was banned from the Olympics at that time because of apartheid policies, a system which denied racial equality to its black and mixed race citizens. Often the athletes themselves disagree with the boycott their country is making. Many of the African athletes were crying in the Games Village and at the airport when they were told by their governments that they would have to leave Montreal.

After the Soviet Union invaded Afghanistan in 1979, forty-five countries led by the United States stayed away from the 1980 Moscow Olympics. Again, many of the athletes did not agree. "I worked too long and too hard not to have hard feelings about missing the Olympics," said Phillip Delesalle, a talented gymnast from Canada. How would you have felt?

Then the Soviet Union led a boycott of the 1984 Los Angeles Olympics. They said it was over security concerns. But everybody knew it was simply revenge for 1980. Romania was one of the few Communist countries that attended the 1984 Games and received the biggest cheer during the opening ceremonies at the Los Angeles Memorial Coliseum.

The 1980 Moscow Summer Olympics were boycotted by forty-five countries.

Many people think that medals won at the boycotted Games are devalued because not all the best athletes were there. Others believe an Olympic medal is an Olympic medal — the winners did the best they could do and the only person you really ever compete against is yourself.

POLITICS AND THE GAMES

Sometimes countries use the Olympics to show that their country and system is best. The Nazis tried to use the 1936 Berlin Olympics to show that they could organize the biggest sporting spectacle ever staged and to prove that their race of people was superior to other races. But that illusion was shattered when American black Jesse Owens won four gold medals in track and field to put the Nazis in their place.

In the most horrible incident at the Olympics, eleven members of the Israeli team were killed by Black September Palestinian terrorists at the 1972 Munich Olympics. The terrorists wanted to make their point at the greatest show on earth — the Olympics. They knew much of the world would be watching the Games and so it afforded them their dream opportunity. They simply climbed over the fence that surrounded the Athletes Village in an era when security was not much thought about at the Games.

A memorial service was held in the stadium the next day. The Olympic flag of peace flying at half mast was a sad sight. Should the Munich Games have been canceled as a sign of respect to those who had died? "No," said International Olympic Committee president Avery Brundage. "The Games must go on." To cancel them would have been to show the terrorists that they had won. Israel's Prime Minister, Golda Meir, agreed with him. She agreed the Games must go on.

Jesse Owens of the U.S. won a spectacular four gold medals in track and field at the 1936 Berlin Olympics but it's not the record for the most golds in a single Games.

The athletes' reaction was mixed. Some felt the Games should go on. Having trained so hard for so long, they were unwilling to give up their dreams, especially over events that were entirely beyond their control. Others were simply too overcome by the horror of the massacre and felt that the rest of the Games should have been cancelled. How do think you would have felt?

Munich changed forever how the Olympics are held. Canadian soldiers with guns and undercover security police were everywhere in Montreal four years later.

But healing does happen — especially in the Olympics.

At the 1992 Barcelona Games, judo athlete Yael Arad won Israel's first-ever Olympic medal. She dedicated the silver medal to the families of those Israeli athletes who died at Munich, with the hope "this will close the circle."

COMMERCIALISM

Many feel the Olympics have lost their true ideals because of commercialism. It costs $40 million to become a major sponsor of the 1996 Atlanta Games. "Jeopardy" and "Wheel of Fortune" are the "official game shows" of the Atlanta Olympics.

Peter Ueberroth pioneered the concept of the private-enterprise Olympics in 1984 at Los Angeles. Those Games made a profit of more than $200 million and have been called the McOlympics. But on the other hand, the taxpayers of Montreal are still paying for the billion-dollar debt caused by the 1976 Games. That money could have built a lot of roads and hospitals. So is commercialism of the Olympics a necessary evil?

The athletes marching into the opening ceremonies of the 1976 Montreal Olympics proudly carrying their flags.

DRUGS

Those who ran the former East German Olympic machine now admit that many of those Games performances were fueled by drugs. The idea was that success in sports would point out that the Communist system was the best. All it did was create an industry for chemists. The East Germans won 411 medals from 1968 to 1988. But who was the real gold medalist in the women's 200 m IM at 1976 in Montreal? Ulrike Tauber of East Germany or second-place-finisher Cheryl Gibson of Canada? And how about in 1980 at Moscow? The winner was East German Petra Schneider. But how is second-place Sharron Davies of Britain supposed to feel about that now?

WIN AT ALL COSTS

The pressure to win can be so great that some nations or individuals will do just about anything to get that precious Olympic gold medal. At the 1976 Montreal Games, modern pentathlete Boris Onishenko of the Soviet Union came in as a gold and silver medalist from two previous Olympics but proved to be a poor electrician. He had wired his electric epee to indicate a score even when he had failed to touch his opponent. He was found out and sent home in disgrace. He was never again seen at any competitions and has become a recluse. He was not very honest. Sometimes money can add to the pressure. Ben Johnson of Canada was going to make between $10 and $15 million by winning the gold medal in the 100 m at the 1988 Seoul Olympics. But he was caught for taking steroids. With that much money at stake, people sometimes do things they shouldn't do to win an Olympic medal.

Many people believe the pressure to win at all costs in the Games is getting out of hand. Just ask Ben Johnson.

CELEBRATE THE SPIRIT

The 1996 Atlanta Summer Olympics mark the 100th anniversary of the modern Olympic era. Many had predicted the movement would never see this anniversary. There have been plenty of problems along the way. But we continue to celebrate the spirit of the Olympics despite its flaws.

Money, advertising and television are powerful forces in the world. And the Olympics reflect that world. Those five rings are the most famous non-religious symbol known to humankind. The Olympics hold up a mirror to the world and reflect its values. The Olympic Games' faults are everybody's faults.

But the same can be said of their good points. They also reflect the good things in all of us. In other words, the Olympics are no different than the people of the world who put them on and compete in them. They bring the world together for a celebration. And that is never a bad thing. The Olympics present the human pageant in all it glory and folly. That is why the Games are a world-wide magnet for critics and boosters alike and why the Olympics remain so interesting and fascinating to people young and old.

Index